SO YOU'RE OFF TO SUMMER CAMP

A TRUNK LOAD OF TIPS FOR A FUN-FILLED CAMP ADVENTURE

By Margaret M. Queen
Illustrated by Margaret H. Matens

Foxglove Press
Nashville, Tennessee

Published by Foxglove Press   P. O. Box 210602   Nashville, TN 37221-0602

Publisher's Cataloging in Publication
(Prepared by Quality Books, Inc.)

Queen, Margaret M.
     So you're off to summer camp: a trunk load of tips for a
fun-filled camp adventure / by Margaret M. Queen; illustrated by
Margaret H. Matens.
     p. cm.
     Includes index.
     Audience: Ages 7-17.
     SUMMARY: Practical guide to summer camps, dealing with
challenges and fears normally encountered in daily life.
     Preassigned LCCN: 93-77129.
     ISBN 1-882959-50-7 (perfect)
     ISBN 1-882959-55-8 (hard)

     1. Summer camps-United States-Juvenile literature.   I.
Matens, Margaret H., ill. II. Title.

GV193.Q441993   796.54'0973
                                           QBI93-447

Printed in the United States of America
Last digit is the print number 9 8 7 6 5 4 3 2 1

Acknowledgements

As I talked to old camp friends, current campers, counselors & camp directors from across the country, many gave suggestions that found their way into the pages of **So You're Off To Summer Camp**.

A sincere thank you to these camp directors who took the time to read the manuscript and share their thoughts: Donald Cheley of Cheley Colorado Camps, Robert Hanson of Mountain Camp II, Ann and Pepe Perron of Camp Nakanawa & Nath Thompson of Camp Carolina.

Thanks, also, to these campers, counselors & former campers who contributed suggestions for this book: Louise Boteler, Rachel Eason, Elizabeth Henri, Elizabeth Hunter, B. J. Jenkins, Courtney Kaminer, Maggie Matens, Murray Matens, Barbara Moate, Sissy Nugon, Jo Parker, Jason Queen, Robin Queen, Lucy Richardson, Beth Seibels, Alex Statland, Beverly Statland, Shannon Waller & Jill Wilmarth.

A special thanks to Margaret Matens for her wonderful illustrations that brought the words to life, and for her many contributions to the text.

And to all who bought this book: A portion of the proceeds from the sale of **So You're Off To Summer Camp** will be donated to a fund to help send children to camp who could not otherwise afford this wonderful experience. You have helped to make this possible.

Introduction

What do you say to your son who's boarding a plane for camp — a camp 2,000 miles and three time zones away? And what advice do you give to your eight-year-old daughter who's thumbing through the camp catalog, wondering what it will be like to spend two whole weeks on her own?

The two of us have spent a combined 30 summers at a number of camps, including over 20 at Camp Nakanawa in Tennessee. We've been campers, counselors, heads of the waterfront and program directors. We've taught horseback riding, canoeing, tennis, arts & crafts, swimming and nature. We've been big sister, teacher and mom to campers from seven to seventeen. Surely, we have trunk loads of advice for our own would-be campers.

Along with the sturdy flashlight, the carefully name-tagged clothes, the already-stamped and addressed post cards, we want our children to tuck into their trunks everything we know that might help make this the perfect experience.

Camp was so vital. It shaped our values, defined the meaning of "friendship," served as the trial and proving ground in those first steps toward independence from home. It taught us self confidence and provided a mainstay of spiritual strength. And it was summers and summers and summers of the most fun imaginable.

So You're Off To Summer Camp is a way to pack all we could into one little book. All the helpful hints we've learned over several decades of camp life. All the observations we've made from watching the struggles and successes of countless novice (spelled N-E-R-V-O-U-S) campers. And all the love we feel for our children as they take part in this special adventure called ... CAMP.

Margaret "Mop" Queen & Margaret Matens

1. Good friends are worth their weight in gummy worms.

2. Hang up your towel on the clothesline after swimming. A wet towel thrown in the corner overnight smells like a dead fish in the morning.

3. Take a sturdy flashlight, one that won't break the first time you drop it. Bring extra bulbs and batteries.

4.
Lots of kids bring a stuffed animal to camp. They're great for hugging when you're feeling lonely.

5. Put on fresh socks and underwear everyday. Just because they still look **white** doesn't mean they are **clean**.

6. The beginning of camp is the time to write most of your letters. That way you'll have time to get lots of replies.

7. If at first camp isn't as wonderful as you expected it to be, give camp (and yourself) three full days before writing anything negative home.

8. Don't worry if you lose your trunk key. One key works for almost every trunk.

9. Do something nice for one of your cabinmates — like making his bed when he is running late. It will make both of you feel important.

10. When you pick out your bunk on the first day, find the one with the least squeaky springs.

11. Learn to play taps. You will always have a special job at camp and ... you'll be the last one to bed.

12. Bring some zany clothes to camp — especially outrageous hats. You will find dozens of uses for them, and the other kids will beat a path to your cabin to borrow things.

13. If you go on a trail ride near a river or lake, be aware that sometimes horses cool off by strolling into the water.

14. Don't pack your really good clothes. The camp laundry may do unusual things to your expensive coordinated outfits.

15. Homesickness will usually strike when you are all alone, when you have nothing to do, or just before lights out. You can avoid these "danger zones" easily: stick with the crowd, volunteer for every activity, and keep a good book handy at bedtime.

16. Every time you write home, find something positive to tell your parents about what you are doing—even if you just say you're making your bed every morning.

18. Learn several good tall tales, jokes or ghost stories. You will be in great demand at bedtime.

19. Carry a change of clothes to camp in case your trunk doesn't arrive on the same day you do.

20. Write home often, even if it's only a post card. Your parents are as anxious for Mail Call as you are.

21. Sometimes the counselors are as nervous as the campers. Let your counselors know you like and support them. Sit on their beds and ask about their girlfriends or boyfriends.

22. Keep a diary.

23. If you'd rather not go to the bathroom alone at night, wake up a friend to go with you. Then your friends will be comfortable asking **you** to go along when **they** need to make the trip.

24. Give new things a chance, whether it's archery or trail rides or a two-day hike. New skills and adventures are what camp is all about.

25. A letter is not finished until it is addressed, stamped and mailed.

Nana Hawkins
6225 Boone Dr.
Baton Rouge, La
70808

26. If you are out in the sun for long hours, use sunscreen. You will pay for harmful sunburns later in life.

27. Eat at least one bite of everything. When you are hungry, even squash tastes pretty good. You will learn to like some new foods, and your parents will be suitably impressed.

28. Only short-sheet your counselor once. The  first time it's funny. The second time it's annoying.

29. Most camp horses know only one speed — slow. There are, however, a few exceptions to this rule. Be honest about how much experience you've had with horses, and the riding counselors will be able to choose a suitable mount for you.

30.
It will be obvious that you are a non-swimmer if you wear your goggles and fins all the way from your cabin to the lake.

31. Pack several card games. Crazy 8s and Slap Jack are popular rainy day pastimes in the cabin.

32. Make friends with people from other cities and states. You may get invited to visit them during the winter.

33. If you're not too sure about going on overnights at camp, you might sleep outside with a friend in your back yard one night before camp starts.

34. Keep your toothbrush, toothpaste, soap and shampoo in a plastic bucket so they can be easily carried to the showers.

35. Use a warm sleeping bag for an extra blanket. It is amazing how cold it can get on a rainy night, especially if your camp is in the mountains. But don't use your sleeping bag in **place** of your sheets.

36. A swim in the lake is not the same as a hot shower with soap and shampoo.

37. It can be slightly embarrassing to bring your parents into the cabin for introductions just when your counselor is changing clothes.

38. When you're not in the game, cheer on your teammates. Show off  your spirit as well as your sports ability.

39. Homesickness is not fatal but it is contagious. Try not to infect the other campers in your cabin. But do tell your counselors — they always know a quick cure.

40. Don't wear flip flops at night. You're likely to stub your toe on a tree root in the dark.

41. A small battery-operated fan is a great way to stay cool in the cabin during Rest Hour.

42. Learn water and boating safety. Your life may depend on it.

43. Be quiet at Rest Hour. Even if the kids don't want to sleep, your counselor probably will. Counselors routinely stay up half the night and will be "crabby" by dinner time if they miss their naps.

45. Bring pictures of your family and pets to tack up by your bed.

46. Your sleeping bags, pack frames, day packs and hiking boots need to be of good quality and durable enough to last several summers. REI (Recreational Equipment Inc.) is an excellent source for children's outdoor equipment. *(Their address can be found at the end of this book.)*

47. Take insect repellent. Mosquitoes seem to know if you left yours at home.

48. If you pack some simple craft materials — leather shoe laces, yarn, beads and embroidery thread — you'll be able to make friendship bracelets and other little gifts for your special pals.

49. When your parents come to see you, share them with your friends whose parents live too far away to visit.

50.
Lots of kids want the adventure of sleeping on a top bunk. But lower bunks have their own appeal. They can be draped with blankets to make a cozy hide-out. And you can entertain yourself by doing gymnastic stunts on the support bar over your head.

51. Bring a good book to read at Rest Hour. Don't let the summer go by without finishing it.

52. If your canoe turns over, stay with it. It will float. Let someone in another boat come to your rescue.

53. Put wax paper between your stamps and envelope flaps so they won't stick together. Or buy the new "can't be licked" adhesive-backed stamps.

54. **Bring more than one bathing suit. Sometimes you swim more than once a day, and it's miserable to have to put on a slimy wet suit.**

55. **When choosing a trunk, remember that kids in your cabin are bound to jump from a top bunk and land on your trunk lid. It's worth it to invest in a sturdy trunk, one that will make it through lots of summers at camp. The Pro-Tech Case Company makes a time-tested trunk. (Their address can be found at the end of this book.)**

56.
Most kids are a little afraid of the dark. If you need to make a trip somewhere at night, invite a buddy to walk with you. It won't seem nearly as dark with two flashlights.

57. Respect the beauty around you — don't litter.

58. Have a counselor show you how to build a campfire without using lighter fluid or kerosene.

59. Don't run around camp barefoot. The camp nurse has plenty to do without bandaging foot wounds.

60. Go to free swim.

61. If you are given a nickname at camp, consider it a compliment. It's usually because you are well liked. If you think the name is degrading, don't let on that it bothers you. Complaining about a nickname is a sure-fire way to make it stick.

62. Shower, shampoo and put on clean clothes before your parents come. Your mom and dad may be fooled into thinking you look that way every day.

63. Don't waste time talking about the TV shows and rock concerts you are missing at home. Focus on what you are gaining at camp.

64. Don't make your counselor wish you lived in another cabin.

65. Listen to the messages at camp worship services.

66. If you feel the urge to play a trick on your counselors, put some of their underwear in Lost and Found. (Pick clothes with names on them, and be sure they are all "found" in the end.)

67. On the first day of camp, arrive early. Pick out your bunk and find the bathroom. After this, help the other campers get settled.

68. Have a positive attitude. It's more contagious than measles.

69. A portable tape player and tapes can be great fun in the cabin and a big help with skits and stunts. But don't plan to play it 24 hours a day.

71. Before you leave home, address and stamp a few envelopes to people you know you plan to write.

72. Yelling "walk" to your horse as he gallops around the ring will accomplish little. Horses respond to your guidance with the reins.

73. Take a picture of a camp sunset and keep it in a frame on your desk during the rainy winter months.

74. Wood ticks can be removed easily. Just see the camp nurse.

75. Respect other people's possessions. If you borrow something, return it ... in the same condition it was in when you borrowed it!

76. Have a counselor show you how to identify poison ivy. The leaves are shiny and grow in groups of three. This knowledge may save you "an ocean of Calamine lotion."

77.
Don't worry about sharing the lake with tadpoles, turtles and other water creatures. They high-tail it out of your area with the first splash.

78. About a week before camp, write yourself a "welcome to camp" letter. Everyone is jealous of campers who get a letter on the very first day.

79. Learn to do some things the old-fashioned way, such as making root beer by boiling sassafras roots.

80. Don't break in your brand new boots during the first five-mile hike at camp ... unless you really happen to like blisters.

81. Don't rush, flush! The next person will appreciate it.

82. Have a set place in the cabin for important things like shoes and flashlight. You may need to find them in a hurry some night.

83. Everyone always sits on the counselor's bed. (But ask first.)

84. Camp directors are warm, loving folks. Feel free to tell them about a problem.

85. Don't let your mother look inside your trunk when she comes to visit. She may faint.

86. Sunglasses get broken at camp.

87. Keep dirty clothes in a laundry bag, not stuffed under your bed.

88. The cabin is a good place for group discussions about growing up and for talking over things that worry you.

89. Work at getting along with the kids in your cabin. You have to work as a team — especially during cabin clean-up.

90. Learn the camp table blessing and then teach it to your family when you get home.

91. Every day, pick one camper you don't really know and get acquainted. Soon you'll know everyone at camp.

92. Shower and change clothes before dinner.

93. Don't brag about family wealth and what your parents do for a living. All that matters at camp is what **you** do.

94.
Contrary to the old wives' tale, bats will **not** fly into your hair and become entangled. No need to sleep with a bathing cap on if you have an occasional bat in your cabin.

95. Make something for each of your family members in crafts class.

96. Print your name and address in big letters on the top of your trunk and place it near your bed. This will identify which bunk is yours.

97. Nothing smells better than bacon and French toast being cooked over a campfire.

98. Never walk behind a horse.

99. Go to sleep at taps. Camp days are full of activities and you need your rest.

100. Check your clothes when they come back from the laundry. Sometimes items in your package belong to another camper, maybe even one from another **camp**.

101. Retrieve tennis balls that go over the fence.

102. Be first in line at Mail Call.

103. Write to your grandparents. They want to hear from you just as much as your parents. And they're more likely to send you a package.

104. Make laughter a big part of your life.

105. Making good friends at camp is more important than being the best swimmer or tennis player.

106. Don't request to be in the same cabin with your best friend from home. You won't make other friends as quickly if you're always a twosome.

107. Give your favorite horse an apple.

108. Make your bed right after breakfast.

109. Don't run down hills. You may start a "human avalanche."

110. Bring toilet paper on overnight trips away from camp. But don't leave little white tufts of paper on the ground. Pack out all your refuse!

111. Wear your flip-flops or aqua socks in the shower to avoid a case of athlete's foot.

112.
Have your name on everything, even your toothbrush. Fifteen percent of all items brought to camp end up in the Lost and Found sometime during the session. Iron-on tapes and permanent laundry pens can be ordered from the Sterling Name Tape Company *(Their address is included at the end of this book.)*

113. Create a "s'more" — marshmallows toasted over a fire then squashed with a chocolate bar between graham crackers.

114. Experiment until you discover when is the best time to get a **hot** shower.

115. Be on time for your activities.

116. Avoid taking hair dryers, electric rollers, electronic games, irons or TVs to camp. You'll find you can survive without things that plug into the wall.

117. Be careful when your horse puts its ears back — it's about to kick.

118. A fun (and harmless) prank is to tie one long string tightly around all the front two chair legs at a dining room table. After the blessing, when the campers try to pull out their chairs and sit down, they'll find their chairs won't budge. And one snip of a knife sets everything right!

119. Nobody enjoys being around a chronic complainer.

120.
A pyramid makes a good group photo. Take two shots —
one from the front and one from the back.

121. Stuff newspaper into the lock opening of your trunk so it won't be accidentally locked.

122. Leave anything really valuable or highly breakable at home.

123. Don't make change in the collection plate.

124. When you shake hands with someone's parents, don't give them a "dead fish." Have a strong handshake and smile like you are pleased to meet them.

125. If you keep striking out, choke up on the bat.

126. Spend time at the nature center. Know the plants and animals that live in your camp environment. Baby snakes like to curl up in your pocket.

127. The camp commissary does not take MasterCard and Visa.

128. Never take a hike in sandals or flip flops.

129. Brush your teeth and use dental floss before you go to bed. Otherwise there may be green slime growing somewhere besides in the lake!

130. If there is someone at camp you can't stand, keep it to yourself. If you make mean remarks about a camper who's not there, your friends may wonder what you say when **they** go off to the showers.

131. If you're uncomfortable changing clothes in front of others, just turn your back and go fast. If you try to change under the covers or in the closet, your cabinmates may make fun of you ... and it will be even more embarrassing.

132. Don't ask your counselors why they were late coming in last night. They <u>never</u> tell.

133. Play tennis with your father when he comes to visit.

134. Don't write home asking your mom to send you a bunch of things you don't really need. She will be stressed out over this request and will write back three letters asking for more complete details and descriptions. By the time you get the package, camp will be over.

135.
Catch a jar of fireflies and sneak them into a cabin. No one will notice them until after lights out, and then the show will begin!

136. Never wear just a towel to the bath house. You'll wish you had worn more when your towel gets yanked off!

137. Swim down and touch the bottom of the lake just once. It may be slimy, but it's good to say you've done it. (Ask permission from the swimming counselor first.)

138. Bring your own baseball glove with you. Camp gloves never feel right.

139. Don't slam cabin doors.

140. Wear your life jacket!

141. Sweeping is the most important job of cabin clean-up.

142. When learning to canoe, concentrate on the "J" stroke. It will ensure that you'll always be able to get back to the dock.

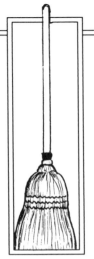

143. Most kids wish their bodies were proportioned differently. Don't think you are the only one who feels this way.

145. Try "spider sniffing." At night, put the end of your flashlight on your nose and look along the beam of light as you walk. Spiders' eyes will glow like twin  jewels in the dark. You'll be amazed at how many eight-legged friends you'll spot.

146. Don't leave tennis balls out in the rain. A soaked tennis ball never bounces the same again.

147. Horse flies don't just bite horses.

148. Don't worry if you  drop your canoe paddle — it will float. If it floats out of reach, you can always paddle your canoe with your hands.

149. Go to the bathroom before going to bed. A "pit stop" right after dinner will not last you through the night.

150. Take soccer or baseball cleats. Everyone will think you are a team starter at home.

151. Don't stomp on ant nests, kick over mushrooms or tear down spider webs. You're just a visitor. This is their permanent home.

152. It's great fun to catch toads, salamanders, butterflies and other wild things. Enjoy getting acquainted and then set them free. Many small creatures will starve in a matter of days.

153. Learn camp songs. Sing them in the shower.

154. Most baby birds learn to fly from the ground. Don't "rescue" a little bird unless it is so young it doesn't have fluffy feathers.

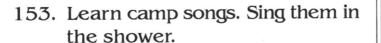

155. Never add to a bed wetter's feelings of embarrassment by making comments. Pretend you don't notice, but be sure your **counselor** knows.

156. Don't spit out food you don't like into your napkin. Some counselors have "napkin check" at the end of a meal.

157. If you have a chance, visit the hayloft of the barn (with permission, of course). It may be the nicest spot in camp.

158.
Sleep out under the stars. Look up and discover the incredible sight of the universe. Find a shooting star and watch a satellite cross the sky.

159. Wear a leather arm protector during archery practice. If not, you could have wrist-to-elbow bruises.

160. Bring grubby clothes for overnight trips.

161. If there is some food you absolutely can't stand, just ask for a small helping and hope no one notices how little you eat. If you make a big Hollywood production of how much you hate oatmeal or broccoli, everyone will be watching to see how much of it you eat.

162. Never leave a campfire unattended and always make sure it's completely out before you leave the campsite.

163. Bathe in bug repellent before a walk in the woods. But don't get it in your eyes — it really burns.

164. Learn at least two of the summer sky constellations besides the Big Dipper and the Little Dipper.

166. In a homesick moment, never ask your parents to come and get you. If you go home early, you will regret it the rest of your life.

167. Store some firewood in a dry area. It's usually your cabin's turn for a cookout after a rainy day.

168. Learn the correct way to fold the flag **before** it's your turn to lead the flag-raising ceremony. You can practice in the cabin with a beach towel.

169. Don't sleep in the same clothes you plan to wear tomorrow even though it speeds up your arrival at breakfast. You will look and feel awful.

170. Don't gripe about the rustic nature of camp. This is not meant to be a stay at an outdoor Marriott.

171. Go to a different camp from all your friends at home. You will double your circle of friends and feel much more adventurous.

172. Changing your mind halfway through a dive will guarantee you a belly flop.

173. "Glow in the dark" galaxy stickers will add pizzazz to your cabin ceiling.

174. Don't worry about your weight at camp. This is not the time to go on a diet.

175. Never skip dessert.

176. Bring duck boots (northwest loafers). Camps can be muddy, especially around the stable.

177. Volunteer to play right field.

178. If you are a bit nervous about learning to swim, remember the most difficult step is putting your head underwater and blowing bubbles out of your nose. After that, the rest is easy.

179. Thank your parents for sending you to camp. It's expensive and, besides, they really miss you.

180. Take the clothes off your clothesline as soon as it starts to rain.

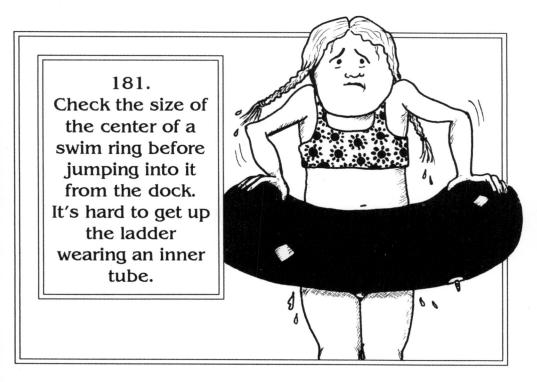

181.
Check the size of the center of a swim ring before jumping into it from the dock. It's hard to get up the ladder wearing an inner tube.

182. Three drops of alcohol in each ear after swimming will help the water evaporate. Otherwise it will gurgle around and drive you nuts!

183. You can't be sure you will win a ribbon at the Horse Show, but it's a sure bet that your horse will pass gas as it prances in front of the judges' stand.

184. If you sit on a rotten log in the woods, you will expose your backside to the home of the chiggers.

185. Soap on a rope is great. It leaves your hands free for washing and shampooing, and you won't lose it in the shower drain.

186. Go to the same camp as your brother or sister. You will appreciate each other more when you're away from home together.

187. Learn to identify the poisonous snakes that live in your camp environment so that you can be comfortable with the multitude of friendly snakes that also live there.

188.
Take time to appreciate your beautiful surroundings. A quiet walk in the woods can be magical. You may spot a bird feather, animal footprints ... or even an arrowhead.

189. Bring more socks to camp than you think you'll need. You may end up changing socks several times a day on rainy days.

190. On trail rides, the horse flies always attack the first few horses. If you're near the back, you'll be fly-less. If you're up front, break off a branch with leaves and use it to brush away the bloodthirsty critters.

191. A poncho keeps you drier than a raincoat, and it's cooler, too.

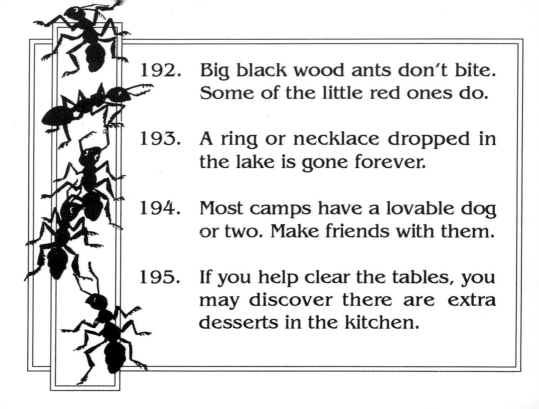

192. Big black wood ants don't bite.
Some of the little red ones do.

193. A ring or necklace dropped in
the lake is gone forever.

194. Most camps have a lovable dog
or two. Make friends with them.

195. If you help clear the tables, you
may discover there are extra
desserts in the kitchen.

196.
A favorite camp prank is running a counselor's underwear up the flag pole — but be sure to pick a counselor with a sense of humor.

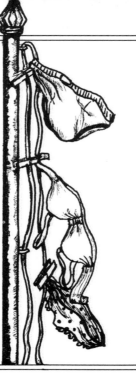

197. Compliment the camp cooks. The better their mood, the better the food!

198. If you're thinking about an early morning escapade, remember this: Camp directors and birds like to get up at the same time every morning.

199. Take pictures of people, not just water, trees and cabins. Get close enough so you'll be able to identify the people when you get the pictures back.

200. Nothing feels worse than stepping on a toad on the tennis court at night when you are barefoot.

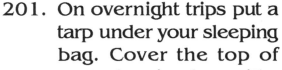

201. On overnight trips put a tarp under your sleeping bag. Cover the top of your sleeping bag with your raincoat or a light tarp so it won't get soaked with the morning dew.

202.
Don't have open containers of food in the cabin unless you want a field mouse banquet under your bunk in the middle of the night.

203. Your first marshmallow will melt and fall into the fire or burst into flames and burn to ashes. It takes a couple of tries to get the hang of it.

204. If you find yourself out at night without a flashlight, pick up each foot high like a prancing horse. It may feel silly but it will save you from tripping on a rock.

205. Don't stare at your counselors when they change clothes in the cabin.

206. Spray insect repellent is very flammable. Don't use it near the campfire.

207. Leave your glasses in the cabin instead of asking the swimming counselor to hold them while you swim. They could get dropped in the lake by accident.

208. You can wear a T-shirt over your bathing suit to cover up an overabundance or a lack of body fat. You can always say it's to keep from getting skin cancer from the sun.

209. If you keep getting holes in the toes of your socks, you may need to clip your toe nails.

210. If you wear a retainer, never fold it in a napkin. You're bound to forget about it and will wind up clawing through the camp garbage to retrieve it.

211. Go swimming with a buddy. If you are on the bottom of the lake, you want to be missed before meal time.

212. Even skinny people can do a great cannon ball.

213. If you pick up a dead stick off the ground to roast your marshmallow or hot dog, the stick will probably go up in flames ... and so will your food.

214. You will get the hiccups only during the table blessing.

215. Have someone take a picture of you with your favorite horse.

216. There are no sharks in the camp lake. Sharks only live in salt water.

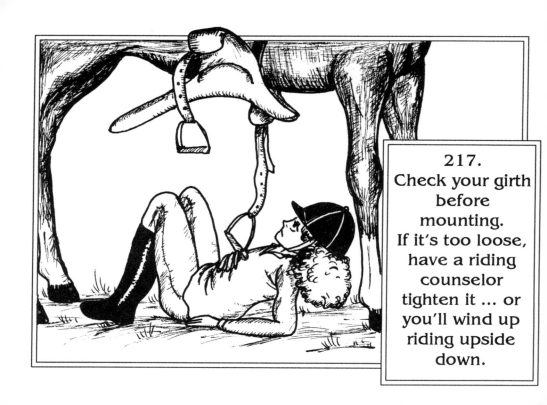

217.
Check your girth before mounting. If it's too loose, have a riding counselor tighten it ... or you'll wind up riding upside down.

218. It's harder to float if you're shaped like a bean pole, but it can be done by breathing deeply and putting your hands up over your head.

219. Volunteer. Whether it's moving hay bales, sweeping out the lodge, carrying firewood or sanding paddles — your willingness to help will be appreciated, you'll meet new kids, and you'll be surprised at how much fun some of these chores become.

220. "What did you bring me?" is the **second** thing to ask your parents on Visitors' Day. **First** ask, "How was your trip?"

221. Camp is a great place to learn outdoor skills ... how to read a map, use a compass, tie knots, build a shelter and do outdoor cooking. Make the most of this opportunity.

222. You may think that talking to your parents on the telephone will make you feel **better**, but it usually leaves you feeling **worse**. Stick with letters.

223. If you play a musical instrument, consider bringing it to camp — unless it's a tuba or a Stradivarius. Camp is a great place to share talents.

224. Pick blackberries in the woods and ask the cooks to make your cabin a pie.

225. Talk to your cabinmates about the places they live. Get their addresses and write to them during the winter months.

226. Make your own "slip and slide" with a piece of plastic and a water hose down by the lake.

227. On a trail ride you will notice how much more cooperative your horse is heading home than it was leaving the barn.

228. Camp is a great place for stomping around in rain boots to see who can make the biggest splash in a giant puddle.

229. Your camp store will sell a few essential items such as stamps, toothpaste, shampoo and film.

231. Go back to the same camp for several summers. You will renew friendships and will enjoy being one of the "old campers" who helps the new kids learn the ropes.

232. Pranks are funny unless ... they damage camp property, hurt someone's feelings, or get played on the same person over and over.

233. If you have a special "skill" — whether it's magic tricks, juggling or burping the alphabet — you'll be an instant success.

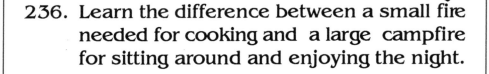

234. Relax. The Tooth Fairy also visits camps.

235. There's a special joy in catching your first fish.

236. Learn the difference between a small fire needed for cooking and a large campfire for sitting around and enjoying the night.

237. The words "thanks" and "please" work at summer camp, too.

238. When you pick up a frog, toad or turtle ... beware! They're scared and their first reaction is to pee on you.

239. If the power goes out and the dark seems scary, just pretend it's a game where someone has turned out the lights.

240. Counselors sometimes get homesick too. And some counselors aren't too fond of spiders and snakes. And some are scared of the dark. They just hide their feelings better than the campers do.

241. If you ever get lost in the woods, **stay put**. The counselors will find you.

242. When you're camping out, put your flashlight in a special place, like inside your shoe. That way you won't have to grope around in the middle of the night to locate it. Your empty shoe can also be a handy place to leave a pair of glasses or a watch for safe-keeping.

243. When you finish canoeing, have your partner help you put the canoe back on the rack. Otherwise, it's sure to become filled with rain. Then it's really heavy!

244.
Getting all six arrows in the target is an accomplishment. **Finding** all six arrows which have **missed** the target can be a challenge, too.

245. Remember to pack some perfume or after shave in case you have a dance with the girls' or boys' camp down the road.

246. If you're worried that you may wet the bed sometime at camp, rest easy. It happens so frequently that counselors are experts at changing the sheets when no one is around. Just be **sure** you tell a counselor. Wet sheets and clothes start to smell very strong after a day or so if they are stuffed into a trunk or laundry bag.

247. On Visitors' Day, take a friend with you to see your parents off. It's a lot easier to wave good-bye to Mom and Dad when you have a friend along for comfort.

248. If it's an extra hot day and you feel overheated, getting your hair wet will make you feel cooler all over.

249. Don't ride horseback in tennis shoes. Your horse will barely feel it when you kick him.

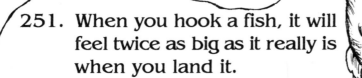

251. When you hook a fish, it will feel twice as big as it really is when you land it.

252. Your bunk should not look like the camp Lost and Found. Your cabinmates will appreciate your tidiness — and so will you when it's time to pack for home.

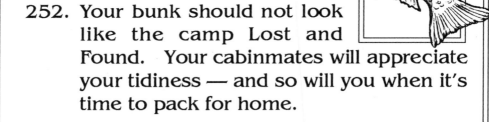

253. Standing up in order to trade bow and stern paddlers is a sure way to turn over your canoe.

254. One of the best poses for your group cabin photo is to line up on the diving board.

255. Try to stay up late enough to watch a full moon come up over the lake.

256. If your camp experience isn't what you think it should be, don't wait until it's over and done before you speak up. Talk to your counselor or the camp director and explain your feelings. They really want you to enjoy your time at camp.

257.
Let little kids
go first,
especially in
line at the
bathroom.

258. When you pack to go home, put your wet bathing suit and towels in a plastic bag. You'll avoid a trunk full of mildewed clothes.

259. If you've always wanted a nickname, camp's your chance! Just introduce yourself to your counselor and new friends by your chosen name, and that's what they will call you.

260. You feel really grown up when you're old enough to take riflery class.

261. Give each member of your cabin a small gift at the end of camp. It will mean more if it's handmade.

262. If your friends take your clothes when you're in the shower, just unhook the shower curtain and wear it back to the cabin. If you don't make a big deal about it, it probably won't happen again.

263. You can get to the top of the biggest mountain if you just think about one step at a time.

264. If you sleepwalk, request a cabin away from the lake.

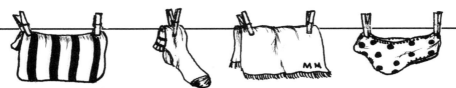

265. Bring clothes pins. Without them, socks and wash cloths stay on the line for about ten seconds on a windy day.

266. Camp laundries are famous for shrinking, bleaching and starching everything.

267. If you know in your heart that you have done your very best, you have been a successful camper even if you are not recognized at Awards Night.

268. Cabin clean-up may seem an unnecessary evil until you consider what your cabin would look like at the end of the session without the threat of inspection!

269. Bullies and braggarts are often kids who are starving for recognition. Try pouring on the attention and praise.

270. On the day of the Horse Show, your horse will have a mind of its own. A horse that has only walked all summer will suddenly go into passing gear.

271.
Listen to the creatures who produce your bedtime lullaby. Learn to identify each sound in your nocturnal orchestra.

272. If someone in your cabin has a birthday, make a big event of it. Draw a special card and have everyone sign it. Decorate the cabin with balloons and streamers. (You can always use toilet paper in a pinch.)

273. Be sure and write down the birthdays of your favorite camp pals so you can mail them birthday cards. *(You can use the address pages in the back of this book.)*

274. Attend camp reunions during the winter.

275. In every competition, there is a winner and a loser. Be good at being both.

276. Plant a tree as a cabin project. Watch its growth for many more summers. It's fun to return and see it 20 years later.

277. The day after you get home, wash all your camp things and pack them back into your trunk. You'll be all ready to go next summer.

278. Don't waste your last days of camp planning how much junk food you'll eat and how late you'll sleep when you're back at home.

279. Always head indoors when you see the first streak of lightning.

280. If you're having conflicts in your cabin, call a bunk meeting with your counselor. Pass around a flashlight and agree that only the person holding the flashlight is allowed to speak. That way each camper gets to talk without being interrupted.

281. If you wake up before reveille, read a book quietly in your bunk. Your fellow campers need their sleep. (So do the counselors!)

282. Everyone does a few belly flops when learning how to dive.

283. If a cabinmate gets sick and has to stay in the infirmary, deliver a get well card signed by everyone in your cabin. It helps to know someone cares... especially when you are not feeling well.

284. Make a cabin wall plaque that includes the date and all the campers' names. It's great to go back years later and find your name.

285. It is sometimes said that camp is not the real world.
Isn't that too bad?

286. A bit of wisdom you learned from a favorite counselor:

287. A piece of advice contributed by the kids in your cabin:

288. See you next summer!

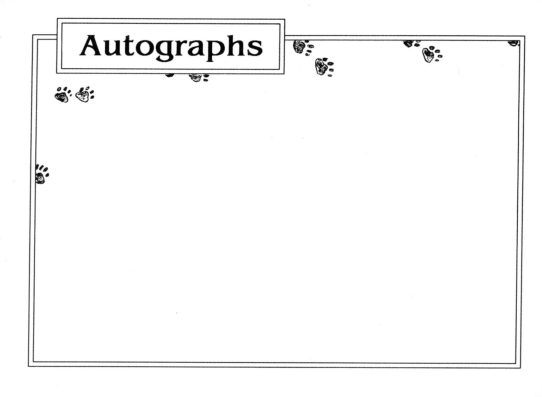

Autographs

Camp Pals I Want to Write

Name _____ **Birthday** _____
Street Address _____
City/State _____ **Zip** _____
Telephone _____

Name _____ **Birthday** _____
Street Address _____
City/State _____ **Zip** _____
Telephone _____

Name _____ **Birthday** _____
Street Address _____
City/State _____ **Zip** _____
Telephone _____

Name _____ **Birthday** _____
Street Address _____
City/State _____ **Zip** _____
Telephone _____

Name _____ **Birthday** _____

Street Address _____

City/State _____ **Zip** _____

Telephone _____

Name _____ **Birthday** _____

Street Address _____

City/State _____ **Zip** _____

Telephone _____

Name _____ **Birthday** _____

Street Address _____

City/State _____ **Zip** _____

Telephone _____

Name _____ **Birthday** _____

Street Address _____

City/State _____ **Zip** _____

Telephone _____

Index

Surpirse Gifts & Lasting Name Tags, Perfect Packs & Sleeping Bags ....

Sterling Name Tape Co.
9 Willow Street
P. O. Box 1056
Winsted, CT 06098-1056
1-800-654-5210

Recreational Equipment Inc.
Sumner, WA 98352-0001
1-800-426-4840

Pro-Tech Case Co.
14506 Parksite Woods
San Antonio, TX 78249
1-210-493-6747

Summer Camp Surprise
Package From:
The Wrinkled Egg ®
P.O. Box 373
Flat Rock, NC 28731
(704) 696-3998

We'd Like to Hear from YOUR Camp ...

What words of wisdom did we forget? Is there a great piece of advice you'd like to share with other campers? What's the most valuable thing a counselor ever told you? A favorite **funny** prank you'd like to tell us about? We'd love to hear from you. And maybe we'll write another camp book and include your idea and your name.

Write: **Foxglove Press**
P. O. Box 210602
Nashville, Tennessee
37221-0602

Be sure to include your name, address, and the name of your camp.

See you around the campfire,

Mop

Margaret "Mop" Queen

Author
Margaret M. Queen
B.S. University of Oklahoma, Physical Education
M.A. University of California, SB, Physical Education
Camper & Counselor — Camp Nakanawa

Illustrator
Margaret H. Matens
B.A. Louisiana State University, English Education
Camper & Counselor — Camp Chattooga , Camp Gulf Park & Camp Nakanawa

Margaret Matens & Margaret Queen

So You're Off To Summer Camp
BOOK ORDER FORM

I would like to order _____ copies of **So You're Off To Summer Camp** at $6.95 per book.

NAME _____

ADDRESS _____

CITY_____ STATE _____ ZIP_____

Make checks payable
& mail to:
Foxglove Press
P. O. Box 210602
Nashville, Tennessee
37221-0602
Unconditional Money Back Guarantee

_____ Books @ $6.95 _____
Add $1.50 for Shipping
.50 for each additional book _____

Tenn. residents add 8.25 % sales tax _____

TOTAL _____